# $\mathcal{S}$hop till you drop, then sit down and buy shoes.

### Written and Illustrated by
### Cathy Guisewite

## Andrews and McMeel
### A Universal Press Syndicate Company
### Kansas City

# Shop till you drop, then sit down and buy shoes.

*T*oday's "must haves."

Tomorrow's "must-have-

been-out-of-my minds."

The next time a man presumes

to have all the answers, send him

to the pantyhose department.

*A* penny saved is a
penny I'm not familiar with.

*I*'d like something

in a nice pump

that will dull the senses

from the ankles up.

$\mathcal{M}$en get dressed.

Women give birth.

*A*n evening out:   $32.00

An evening in:   $493.00

Based entirely on footwear,

future civilizations will assume

that women ruled the world.

*I*nstinctively, she sensed

the whole evening would have

gone differently if only she'd

bought the matching ankle boots.

I love sales.  I love

anything that involves reduction.

If the malls really

believed in customer service,

they'd rent storage lockers.

Do you have anything exactly like this, except with shoulder pads, and that comes down to my knees?

The mid-life crisis:

this year's gift-with-purchase.

shop,

therefore I am.